D0885523

Desirée Mays
Opera Unveiled

2008

To Cynthia r Howard -
Enjoy and many thanks!
Desirée

♪

ART FORMS INC.
Santa Fe · Salt Lake City

Art Forms Inc.
Opera Unveiled 2008 © by Art Forms Inc.
Text copyright © Desirée Mays

Cover design and layout by Pieter Hull
Rear cover photograph by Carolyn Wright
Copyeditors Jo Ann Baldinger
and Vanessa Caminiti

First edition

ISBN 978-0-9707822-7-4

To order individual copies of *Opera Unveiled 1999 - 2008*
please send a check for $17 (postage included) to:
Art Forms, Inc., 31 Valencia Loop
Santa Fe, New Mexico 87508
Fax: (505) 466 1908
Email: dmmays@gmail.com

Contents

Billy Budd

Benjamin Britten

*A rtists are artists because they have an exquisite
sensitivity – a skin less, perhaps, than other people... So
when you hear of an artist doing or saying something strange
or unpopular, think of that extra sensitivity, that skin less;
consider for a moment whether he may not after all be seeing
a little more clearly than ourselves, before you condemn him.
It is a proud privilege to be a creative artist, but it can also
be painful.*

– Benjamin Britten, July 28, 1951

"Billy Budd, king of the birds," cries the exuberant young
sailor, flying free of life's cares, free to love, free to die,
soaring above men's petty jealousies, desires, and laws, a
truly unfettered spirit. For this supreme joy in life, Billy had
to die, condemned by two men, one motivated by frustrated
malice, the other by a sense of duty to the law.

Hermann Melville, one of America's great writers, wrote
Billy Budd in 1891, leaving the end of the book, the poem
"Billy in the Darbies," unfinished at his death. The 351-page
manuscript lay undiscovered in a tin breadbox for many years
and was not published until 1924. Coming at the end of a long,
turbulent career, *Billy Budd* expressed much of the pain and
confusion in Melville's dark, questing soul. The novel centers

on the relationships of men on board a British man-o'-war, the HMS *Indomitable,* fighting the French in 1797.

Melville knew about life on ships. He first went to sea at the age of 17, voyaging to the South Seas and writing of his adventures there. In the course of his travels, Melville was aware of homosexuality in the communities in which he found himself, both at sea and on land, so it is not surprising that many of his books describe close relationships among men. Given his Puritan background and the mores of the day, Melville had, of necessity, to repress any homoerotic feelings of his own, but he clearly enjoyed the company of men at home, abroad, and at sea. Though there is no explicit depiction of any sexual liaison in Melville's books, many of them describe and refer to deep friendships and love between men.

Billy Budd was derived from a variety of sources. While serving on the American frigate *United States*, Melville became friends with a man called Jack Chase, captain of the foretop and loved by all on board. Melville made him the hero of *White Jacket* and dedicated *Billy Budd* to Chase, whose rugged good looks and lively spirit served as a model for Billy.

A personal tragedy may also have provided impetus for *Billy Budd:* Melville's son Malcolm committed suicide at age 18, and Melville mourned his death even as Captain Vere, filled with anguish and guilt, mourned the death of young Billy. Aspects of Melville may also be found in the character of John Claggart, a man filled with longing for what could not be, feeding on his own inability to be true to himself.

Melville knew the story of a young seaman who, in 1846, struck an officer and was condemned to hang by a court-martial convened by the ship's commander. As the young sailor died he was reported to have forgiven the captain for his sentence, saying, "I honor you for it, God bless that flag!" In another incident, on the USS *Somers*, three men were hanged from the yardarm for planning a mutiny. One of the officers in that court-martial was Melville's cousin. Melville himself had been part of a shipboard uprising in Tahiti, so he knew well the causes of mutiny.

Mutiny was an ever-present concern to the Royal Navy at the end of the 18th century. England was at war with the revolutionary government of France, and *Billy Budd* is set on a warship whose mission was to defeat and sink French ships. Conditions on these battleships were appalling: the food was bad, discipline was strict, and floggings the order of the day for the smallest misdemeanors, including the accidental knocking down of an officer by a seaman as happens in *Billy Budd*. Brutal floggings, witnessed by the whole crew, were a means of maintaining control over men who typically had been forced into the service.

Two mutinies in 1797 – one at Spithead, near Portsmouth, the other at Nore in the Thames estuary – had sparked fears in the Navy that such incidents would lead to revolution, as had happened in France. The Spithead mutiny, over living conditions on the ships and requests for pay raises, ended peacefully with concessions made, while the Nore mutiny resulted in the hanging of 20 men who took a political stand in addition to airing their grievances. Most of the men on British warships had been impressed – taken forcibly from the land or another ship and made to serve on Navy vessels. Three men, including Billy, are impressed to join the HMS *Indomitable* at the start of the opera.

Melville's tale of the Handsome Sailor and the hard life of men at sea appealed at once to the sensitive, compassionate Benjamin Britten, who had been a conscientious objector during World War II. Britten and his lifetime partner, tenor Peter Pears (for whom the role of Captain Vere was composed), were living in their home in Aldeburgh, on the east coast of England, when work commenced on *Billy Budd* in 1948. Britten asked the eminent writer E. M. Forster to write the libretto. It was Forster who, in a radio broadcast some years earlier, had introduced Britten to the story of *Peter Grimes*. Britten had wanted to collaborate with the older writer since that time. Forster, who by then was 70, had never written a libretto, so Eric Crozier, a close friend who had collaborated with Britten on several operas, joined the team.

Five versions of the text were developed before Britten started composition. Forster, then living in rooms at Cambridge University, was excited about the project. His writing career had drifted into an extended calm in which he found himself unhappy both personally and professionally, and he welcomed the task of transforming Melville's *Billy Budd* into a libretto and working with the young composer Benjamin Britten. He wrote the opening lines of the Prologue at once, lines which remained unchanged: "I am an old man who has experienced much...."

The libretto was written in prose, with Crozier and Forster meeting frequently in Aldeburgh to discuss the transition from novel to libretto. Once the text was completed, Britten began composition of what came to be described as a "stern and beautiful opera" that has "a perfection of its own ... there is about this music a touch of precariousness, a touch of strangeness." The premiere, held at Covent Garden in 1951, was very successful.

Billy Budd, originally in four acts, then revised by Britten to two, begins and ends with the Honorable Captain Edward Fairfax Vere as an old man, retired from the Navy and looking back on his career and his encounter with Billy Budd. Vere tells us he has read, studied, and pondered in an effort to "fathom eternal truth." His very name means Truth, Vere from *veritas*. Good, he believes, always has some flaw, "some fault in the angelic song, some stammer in the divine speech." He questions, "What have I done? Who has blessed me? Who saved me?"

The scene fades back to 1797 on board the HMS *Indomitable,* commanded by a younger Edward Fairfax Vere. We see the sailors holystoning the decks, singing as they work, "Heave, o heave away." Holystones were soft, brittle sandstone blocks used to scour and whiten the decks of ships. The men are forced to keep up the pace by aggressive first and second mates. The Novice accidentally collides with the Bosun, who threatens a flogging if it happens again. The ship is busy, alive with action. The Novice runs across the deck, slips, and falls; the Bosun orders 20 strokes, and the terrified Novice is dragged off.

A boarding-party boat approaches the *Indomitable* with three new recruits, impressed from a passing merchant ship called the *Rights o' Man.* Officers and the recruits come aboard. John Claggart, the Master-at-Arms, is sent for to question them. The first recruit, Red Whiskers, protests they have no right to impress him. Claggart insists on the man's name, age, and trade, and he is assigned to the forepeak. The second man, a weaver, is also sent for'ard. Claggart questions the third recruit: "Your name?" "Billy Budd, sir." He doesn't know his age, says he is an able seaman. He can't read, but he can sing, he tells Claggart. The officers are pleased; here at last is a better prospect. Claggart asks, "Where is your home?" Billy struggles to answer, but stutters and stammers. The officers note there is always some flaw, in Billy's case a stammer. At last he explains he was a foundling. Claggart appears to agree that Billy is a find, "A beauty. A jewel, a pearl of great price." Billy is assigned to the foretop, where strong young sailors work pulling in the enormous canvas sails at the top of the tall masts.

The exuberant Billy is thrilled and sings of his happiness to be high among the birds, looking down on the decks and the waves, working, helping, and sharing with his new mates. He then turns to the merchantman he has left and cries out, "Farewell *Rights o' Man!*" to the consternation of the officers, who see this as a rebellious act invoking Thomas Paine's incendiary book and the recent mutinies. The decks are cleared. Claggart has taken note of Billy's words. In an aside he tells us he has studied man's weaknesses and apprenticed himself to "this hateful, accursed ship" for reasons that are never disclosed. He despises the officers. Claggart, who has the unenviable job of maintaining order on board, is generally disliked by officers and men alike. He calls Squeak, his informer, and orders him to spy on Billy and make trouble for him.

The Novice and his friends enter to a dirge. The boy has been beaten badly and is suffering both pain and shame; all are "lost forever on the endless sea," he cries in despair. Billy, observing his punishment, pities the young sailor. An old seaman, Dansker, calls Billy "Baby" and tells him floggings can happen to anyone, anytime, for little reason. Whistles blow; it's time to get aloft. Claggart approaches Billy, calls him "Beauty," and orders him to "take off that fancy neckerchief." (In a filmed production, Claggart pulls the neckerchief off Billy's neck and almost caresses it before thrusting it back at him.) The other sailors warn the young foretopman to steer clear of Claggart, but Billy sees no harm in him. Billy asks about the Captain of the ship. "Starry Vere, we call him," the men reply. They love and respect the man who is a "giant in battle, who is brave and good." Billy is delighted: "Goodness is best and I'm for it, Starry Vere, and I'm for you."

A week later Vere invites his officers, Mr. Redburn and Mr. Flint, to join him for a glass of wine. They arrive, toast the King, and then rally one another in anticipation of a confrontation with a French ship. They don't like the French: "Don't like their Frenchified ways. Don't like their bowing and scraping, their hoppity skippity ways, or their lingo" – a rare moment of levity in the opera before the conversation becomes serious. They feel the danger of mutiny, of French ideas infecting the British fleet. Following the Nore mutiny,

Vere says, they must be vigilant, "be on our guard." They remember Billy calling out "The rights o' man," but Vere sees no danger in Billy, only "youthful high spirits." As the officers enjoy their wine, the men can be heard singing a shanty from below decks. The officers leave and Vere takes up his book, then pauses to listen to the singing of the men.

Donald, Red Whiskers, and Billy lead a sea shanty, with the others joining in the chorus, "We're off to Bermuda, the Sultan of Judah can eat barracuda, including the weevils and all." Dansker says he is too old to join in, he only wants a chew of tobacco. Offering to fetch his own, Billy leaves, only to return moments later, furious because he has caught Squeak going through his belongings. The angry Billy stammers, unable to speak. The two men fight. Billy knocks Squeak down just as Claggart arrives on the scene "How did this start?" he demands. Dansker explains. Claggart has Squeak arrested, then turns to Billy and says, "Handsomely done, and handsome is as handsome did it, too."

Later, Claggart walks the deck thinking about Billy. He sings a soliloquy that brings to mind Iago's Credo in *Otello*, revealing his dark thoughts. Claggart hates Billy for his "Beauty, Handsomeness, Goodness." He wishes they had never met. "What choice remains to me? I am doomed to annihilate you, destroy you, wipe you off the face of the earth. I will mutilate and silence the body where you dwell, it shall hang from the yardarm." Claggart's unprovoked hatred is palpable, incomprehensible. He is bent on destruction and ends his aria, "If love still lives and grows strong where I cannot enter, what hope is there for me?"

He sees the Novice, whom he has summoned, and instructs him to tempt a fellow shipmate with gold coins. Upon learning that Billy is the target, the Novice cries out that he cannot hurt Billy, the "one we all love." When Claggart threatens a further flogging, however, the Novice gives in and takes the gold. He makes his way below decks to the hammock where Billy lies, dreaming of being under the sea. The Novice wakes him and tells him the impressed men have formed a gang and want Billy to help them. He shows Billy the gold. Now fully awake, Billy realizes what is being asked of him – and stammers. He threatens the Novice, who flees in terror. Dansker appears. Billy tells him he was asked to mutiny. Guessing what is going on, Dansker warns, "Jemmy Legs [Claggart] is down on you," but Billy doesn't believe him, for Claggart has always been kind to him. The act ends with Billy's affirmation of faith in Claggart and Dansker's warning. There is more than an echo here of a line from *Peter Grimes,* "Grimes is at his exercise [of cruelty]" in Dansker's repeated line, "Jemmy Legs is down on you," ending the act with a sense of dark foreboding.

Act II begins on the main deck some days later. The ship is shrouded in mist, providing little hope that the enemy will be sighted that day, and the men are growing restless. Claggart requests an interview with the Captain. Obsequiously, he informs Vere that he has served his country and his ship well but now there is danger and he feels it is his duty to report it. At this moment the mist lifts and the ship leaps into action – a Frenchman has been sighted! The entire crew prepares for battle as the *Indomitable* gives chase. "A froggy, our first fight! We'll blow her from the water!" the men cry. There is tremendous excitement on board and in the score as the ship prepares for battle. A cannon is fired, but the shot falls short for the enemy is out of range. The wind dies and the mist descends once more. It is over. The disappointed crew is dismissed to quarters.

Claggart returns to Vere, stating there is a dangerous man on board who plans mutiny. Vere demands proof. Claggart produces the gold coins, which he claims Billy offered to the Novice. When Vere hears that the accused is Billy he is amazed. The confrontation between the two men intensifies, with Claggart insistent but deferential and Vere incredulous.

Claggart suggests that his Captain only sees Billy's exterior, "the flower of masculine strength and beauty" – odd words for a master-at-arms to use about a sailor. Insisting that the boy is good, Vere decides to call Billy so that Claggart can accuse him to his face.

Billy almost bounces in, believing Vere is going to promote him: "I'd serve you well, you'd be safe with me, I'd die for you," the boy tells his captain. Vere explains he has been summoned about another matter and calls the Master-at-Arms. Claggart takes a vicious delight in telling Billy, "I accuse you of disaffection and insubordination of aiding our enemies. You are a traitor, I accuse you of mutiny." Billy is so shocked he is unable to speak. The kindly Vere lays a hand on his shoulder and says: "Take your time, boy." Billy struggles to speak, then finally lashes out with his fist, striking Claggart on the forehead. Claggart falls, and Vere realizes at once the blow was fatal. "Fated boy, what have you done?" He sends Billy to a nearby cabin. "Beauty, handsomeness, goodness [the same words used by Claggart] coming to trial. How can I condemn him? How can I save him? It is not his trial, it is mine." He knows all to well the monstrous decision that lies ahead.

Vere summons his officers and briefly, objectively, tells them what happened. All three at once take the boy's part. Vere informs them he is calling a drumhead court, a court-martial hearing. Vere will give testimony as the witness. Billy is brought in to answer the charges. He denies the accusation of planning mutiny: "Never, never could I do those foul things." He explains that when confronting Claggart his tongue would not work, "so I had to say it with a blow, and it killed him." Billy then appeals to Vere, "Captain Vere, save me! I'd have died for you." But Vere is silent as Billy is led away.

The officers understand that, given the Mutiny Act, the King's Regulations, and the Articles of War, they have no choice but to hang Billy. They look to Vere for guidance, but he refuses to offer it. "Pronounce your verdict," he orders.

Billy is found guilty and sentenced to die by hanging from the yardarm at dawn. Vere accepts the verdict and then, when the officers leave, wrestles with his conscience. Legally he has done the "right" thing by sentencing Billy: "Death is the penalty for those who break the laws of earth," but he is about to destroy goodness itself: "The angel of God has struck and the angel must die through me. I am the messenger of death."

An extraordinary series of 34 chords accompanies Vere as he walks to the cabin where Billy is held, opens the door, and disappears inside. These chords, scored for full orchestra, each different in sonority and pitch, are related to the notes that form a vast harmonized F major arpeggio. They will be heard again; when Billy sings in his final aria that he is strong, the mere chords appear to give him fortitude. This quiet orchestral interlude, set amid the violence of what has gone before, is a moment of profound beauty and truth, a moment beyond Fate, when the choices have been made. We are not told what happens in the interview, only [in Melville] that Vere comes out looking shaken and Billy somehow seems to have gained strength from it. Melville writes that "something of healing" passed between Billy and Vere. The chords stand guard over an interview in which Fate itself is overcome as both men agree, on some level, to accept what has to be done.

A brief musical transition shifts the scene to the gundeck, where Billy is held in irons between two cannons, awaiting execution. In his aria, closely based on the poem that ended Melville's story, "Billy in the Darbies" (darbies being irons or shackles), the chords of the interview are interwoven into his music, suggesting that Billy's strength has come from whatever occurred between the two men. Billy sees the moonshine through the porthole. "Ay, ay, all is up," he sings, "and I must up too." He thinks of the last food and drink a messmate will bring him and wonders who will run him up. He imagines a friendly hand at the plank before they send his body to the deep. "They'll lash me in my hammock, drop me deep, fathoms, fathoms down. I'm sleepy and oozy weeds about me creep."

Dansker arrives with a tot of rum and a biscuit, a final communion. Billy asks him to prevent the men from making trouble on his behalf. "They hated Jemmy Legs," Dansker tells the condemned boy. "They swear you shan't swing. They love you." Billy says he had to strike down Claggart and Vere had to strike him down – it's Fate. He asks Dansker to have the crew help Starry Vere. Dansker leaves. Billy says his farewells, then suddenly sights "a sail in the storm that's not Fate and I'm contented. I've seen where she's bound for. She has a land of her own where she'll anchor forever. Don't matter now being hanged. I'll stay strong and that's enough."

The final scene is set at first daylight. Silently, the entire crew assembles on deck in what can only be described as a funeral march. The fugal orchestration of this scene intensifies the emotions of the men lined up to witness Billy's execution. The First Lieutenant reads the Articles of War and Billy's sentence. The men stand still, waiting. Billy cries out, "Starry Vere, God bless you." The men and officers repeat the line. Billy is led away. The hanging is described by Melville:

> *It chanced that the vapoury cloud hanging low in the East, was shot through with a soft glory as of the fleece of the Lamb of God seen in mystical vision; and simultaneously, watched by the wedged mass of upturned faces, Billy ascended; and ascending, took the full rose of the dawn.*

As Billy is hanged, a wordless chorus of rage and rebellion rises from the assembled crew. The officers order the decks cleared at once and, from force of habit, the men slowly obey.

The light fades, and we are returned to Vere as the old man of the Prologue. He recalls how the sea birds enshadowed

Billy with their wings as he dropped into the sea, their harsh cries a requiem. He accuses himself: "I could have saved him. What have I done? But he has saved me and blessed me and the love that passes understanding has come to me." Then, repeating Billy's music, Vere sings, "I was lost on the infinite sea but I've sighted a sail, the far-shining sail, and I'm content." As Vere relives that last interview, his and Billy's themes are joined, and Vere finds, at last, the same strength, love, and freedom that Billy experienced in the final hours of his life.

Britten uses a full orchestra for *Billy Budd* and makes much use of brass, percussion, and woodwind in the score. The haunting opening chords depict a calm sea under the first gray streaks of dawn. In a quiet oscillating motion a conflict is heard, in which Britten uses minor-within-major thirds to introduce the unsettling little melodic phrase that recurs many times in the work. He also uses the opposition of the chords of B flat major and B minor, symbolizing the irreconcilability of opposites and providing a thread of disunity for the whole score. This undermining of one key by its neighboring semitone increases the tension in the drama. It is heard when the Novice tries to bribe Billy in music that hovers between F and F sharp minor. When Billy is hanged, the sound of the sailors' roar in B is silenced by the officer's command for order in B flat.

There are many elements in this tale, many ways to interpret it. Is Billy a Christian, even a Christ-like figure, with Vere as Pontius Pilate sentencing him to death while knowing in his heart it is wrong? Billy embodies love; he loves everyone and, in return, is loved by all but Claggart. Just before his hanging, he forgives and blesses even as Christ did, not from a cross, but with a noose tightening around his neck. His last supper is a biscuit and rum shared with a friend who assures Billy that his shipmates are behind him, they love him and will attempt to save him, even as the disciples promised Christ. The far-shining sail that Billy, and later Vere, sees in the distance is a message of hope. Forster saw the white sail as Love, the means of salvation from a hostile Fate.

There is an element of homosexuality in both Melville's novel and the opera, a depiction of the love that can exist between men who are isolated from their families and homes on a ship that is truly a microcosm of the world itself. Melville knew this world. Forster, living at the time of Oscar Wilde's trial, knew this world also; he found happiness in male relationships but was forced to keep them secret. Britten shared a true love relationship with Peter Pears, though even as late as the mid-20th century homosexual relationships were illegal in England. These men, both the creators of the tale and the characters in the story, were all familiar and comfortable with a world in which men lived with and loved one another.

Billy is the archetypal object of desire. If he walked into a room all heads, both male and female, would turn at his physical beauty and his inner radiance. Theodor Uppman, the first Billy Budd, said that Britten himself described Billy as having this "inner radiance." There is no suggestion of sexual encounters in either the book or opera, but there are many references to the love and admiration of one man for another. In Melville, Vere describes Billy as "a fine specimen of the *genus homo*, who in the nude, might have posed for a statue of the young Adam before the fall." Billy hero-worships Vere, seeing in him perhaps the father he never had. He wants to be near him. He tells Vere, ironically, that he would die for him. Billy sees only good in people, in spite of catching Squeak rifling through his belongings and being incited to mutiny by the Novice, both plots originating with Claggart, the vicious nemesis whom he so mistakenly trusts.

Melville tells us: "What it was that first moved [Claggart] against Billy, was his significant personal beauty." Claggart's glance would "follow the cheerful Sea Hyperion with a settled meditative and melancholy expression, his eyes suffused with incipient tears. Claggart could have loved Billy but for fate and ban." Filled with dark desires, Claggart has to find a solution. In writing to Britten about Claggart's Act I soliloquy, Forster was unequivocal. "I want passion" he wrote, "– love constricted, perverted, poisoned, but nevertheless flowing down its agonized channel; a sexual discharge gone evil." Claggart, in Melville, is the Serpent to Billy's Adam. His attraction to Billy brings with it self-loathing and, he tells us in his aria, a determination to destroy the boy who evokes such feelings. Claggart states he has no choice; Fate requires him to destroy the object of his dark desire.

Captain Edward Fairfax Vere is a man of books and culture, but also a leader, a man of action in dangerous times. His crew is entirely loyal to the man they call Starry Vere. Though Vere and Billy do not meet in the opera until the scene of Claggart's denunciation, Vere is very aware of the young sailor about whom he gets such good reports. He sees Billy as an angel of God, and at the moment of Claggart's death knows at once the terrible dilemma that lies before both himself and the boy. Vere's struggle with his conscience and his flawed decision is at the heart of the story, making Vere, not Billy, the central character. On one hand he must abide by the rules; it is his supreme duty to obey the law, to be a commander of men at a time of war; on the other, he knows that the sentence, while legally justified, is morally unjust. Once the decision is made, however, he stands by it and chooses to give Billy the verdict himself. What happens behind the closed doors of the cabin where Billy awaits him is a mystery, veiled from our sight and presented, in a masterstroke, by Britten in those 34 haunting chords. Perhaps, as Melville suggested, Vere "may in the end have caught Billy to his heart even as Abraham may have caught young Isaac on the brink of resolutely offering him up in obedience to the exacting behest." The paternal Vere could have held the boy like a son, as perhaps Melville wanted to hold the son who died at the same age as Billy.

The Santa Fe production will faithfully follow Britten's directions. The set is a cross-section of a great sailing vessel with the main deck center stage, and the poop deck, with the helm where the officers stand, upstage of that. The sides of the ship run along the sides of the stage, the rigging is secured from the rails and climbs to the top of the mast. A crow's nest encircles the center of the main mast. A great sail is furled high above the stage and only unfurls once during the opera.

So, in this all-male opera we meet, see and hear Billy, a naive young man whose inner radiance attracts all who encounter him; the evil Claggart who destroys Billy in order to destroy his own dark demons; and Vere a troubled, paternal figure. The paths of these three men cross on board ship at sea and, in a truly gripping score, Benjamin Britten leads us to a new understanding of the meaning of "Beauty, Handsomeness, and Goodness."

Characters

Billy Budd, seaman	Baritone
Edward Fairfax Vere, Captain	Tenor
John Claggart, Master-at-Arms	Bass
Dansker, old seaman	Bass
Novice	Tenor
Squeak	Tenor

Many officers, seamen, and a large chorus

Bibliography

Fuller, Michael. "Far-shining sail," *Musical Times,* Summer 2006.

Kennedy, Michael. *Britten*, Master Musicians series. Oxford University Press, 1993.

Libretto from *Billy Budd* CD. Chandos Records 9826(3), 2000.

Melville, Herman. *Billy Budd, Foretopman*. New York: Ventura Books, 1980.

Opera News, Billy Budd edition, April 19, 1980.

Personal communication, Bruce Donnell, opera director, Santa Fe, 2007.

Radamisto

George Frideric Handel

G eorge Frideric Handel led a full and colorful life, to put it mildly. Appointed court composer to George, Elector of Hanover, in 1710, Handel then proceeded to spend most of his time in England, quickly achieving recognition there with his opera, *Rinaldo*. He was in London when Queen Anne died; she was succeeded, in 1714, by none other than Handel's abandoned patron, now George I. When the new king arrived in London, Handel was in disgrace.

The differences between the two men were resolved in a rather unconventional way in 1717, when the king expressed a desire to enjoy a concert on the Thames. It was duly reported that, on the evening of 17 July, "The king repaired to his barge with members of the court. Next to the king's barge was that of the musicians, about 50 in number, who played all kinds of instruments. Unbeknownst to the king, the music had been composed by Handel, his former employee. His Majesty approved of the music so much that he caused it to be repeated three times. The number of barges and, above all, of boats desirous of hearing [the music] was beyond counting." Thus Handel's famous *Water Music* healed the rift between the king and his errant court composer.

During this period the nobility of London, having

discovered the joys of Italian Baroque opera during the Grand Tour in Europe, determined to raise money to found an Academy of Music. The intention of the Academy was to present a constant supply of operas composed by Handel. Subscriptions were sold, the king gave his name to the project, and the Royal Academy came to life as the King's Theatre in the Haymarket. Handel, as the first artistic director, was instructed to contract leading European singers for the company. He lined up the best, including many of the most famous castrati; one of them, Senesino, was immediately engaged as the leading *primo uomo* for the Academy.

Radamisto was first presented in April 1720 as part of the opening season at the King's Theatre and was an immediate success. Handel dedicated the work to George I, acknowledging the King's royal favor. The opera was performed again in December, this time with Senesino replacing the soprano who had sung the title role at the premiere.

Handel devoted the next eight years of his life to the Royal Academy, achieving artistic triumphs that were unprecedented, and firmly establishing London as the center of the operatic world. The fortunes of the Academy, however, rose and fell. Handel himself was in dire financial straits in 1728, when the Academy was forced to close temporarily as subscriptions and the singers' contracts ran out. The battles among the singers, divas, and castrati had become increasingly unmanageable, and London's love affair with the Baroque, which had lasted less than a decade, was winding down.

At the height of the Academy's woes, John Gay presented his *Beggar's Opera*, a ballad opera, or "burlesque." Nothing like this had been seen before, and London audiences were primed for change. *The Beggar's Opera* became the rage of London and, to this day, remains one of the most frequently performed works from the English repertoire of that period. This burlesque bore no resemblance whatsoever to Baroque opera; in fact, it parodied the operas of the Royal Academy, their conventions, and the artificiality of Baroque style. *The Beggar's Opera* took as its source a series of witty, irreverent popular songs from England, Scotland, and Ireland and transported the action from the noble palaces and extravagant scenery of the Baroque to a setting of scurrilous low life. John Gay's parody amused the Londoners who flocked to performances, reveling in the satire of their once-sacred Baroque form. This was a turning point for opera. Handel went on to compose more operas, but ultimately turned to oratorios and other works with which he continued to enjoy success. (*The Messiah* was just one of these later compositions.)

For Handel, the most important element in opera was song. Ironically, this gave free rein to the tyranny of singers whose exorbitant vanity, feuding, and competitiveness destroyed the Royal Academy and put an end to a brief but glorious era of opera in the 1720s. Handel's operas, however, have withstood the test of time because of his ability to express so well the emotional states of his characters. His arias are expansive and always allied to the drama. Handel makes an instrument of the voice; as Peter Conrad states in *A Song of Love and Death,* "Flowing from inside the body, the Handelian voice constitutes and carpets the landscape."

The sources of *Radamisto* can be traced to a brief account, in Tacitus' *Annals of Imperial Rome,* of an incident that took place in Asia Minor around 51 AD. Radamistus, escaping from Armenia with his pregnant wife Zenobia, attempts to kill her at her behest because she cannot undertake the long ride on horseback and prefers death to capture. Radamisto leaves her for dead on the banks of the Araxes river. She is later found alive by shepherds, who bring her to the court of Tiridate, the Armenian king, where she is treated well, in accordance with her royal status. This incident appears in

Act II of Handel's opera, when Zenobia begs Radamisto to kill her, but with a very different outcome.

From this germ of a story came the opera, *L'amor tyrannico* (Tyrannical Love), composed by Francesco Gasparini for a production in Venice in 1710. A new adaptation of the libretto was written by Domenico Lally in the newly elevated style of the Baroque. Finally Nicola Haym, librettist for the Royal Academy in London, strengthened the libretto for Handel to give emphasis to the noble endurance of the three leading characters: Zenobia, Radamisto, and Polissena.

The story focuses on the trials and tribulations of two magnificent women, both faithful wives: Zenobia, whose husband, Radamisto, loves her, and Polissena, whose husband, Tiridate, lusts after Zenobia. Tiridate lays siege to the city of Thrace, planning to kill the king Farasmane and his son Radamisto and carry off Zenobia for himself. While escaping from the burning city, Zenobia begs her husband to kill her rather than let her fall into Tiridate's hands. Radamisto attempts to do so but cannot, so she jumps into the river Araxes and is assumed drowned. Radamisto is captured. Unbeknownst to him, Zenobia is rescued from the river and brought to Tiridate's court.

In a parallel plot, Polissena (wife of Tiridate and sister of Radamisto) finds herself innocently enmeshed in a web of intrigue. The husband she loves rejects her because of his desire for Zenobia. Polissena is loved from afar by Prince Tigrane, who is aware of her unhappiness. He encourages Polissena to leave Tiridate, but she chooses to remain faithful to her husband, telling Tigrane that duty forbids this course of action. Later, in an attempt to help the beleaguered brother and sister, Tigrane brings the captured Radamisto to Polissena. Radamisto now insists that Polissena allow him to kill the tyrant Tiridate, but once again Polissena stands by her husband and will not let that happen. When there seems to be an impasse on all fronts, Tiridate's army revolts, and he is left defenseless. Radamisto is reunited with his beloved Zenobia, he forgives everyone, and they all more or less return from whence they came, with honor intact and noble sentiments expressed all round as the opera ends with a dance of celebration.

This is but a very brief summary of a complex plot, which is easy enough to follow as one watches it unfold.

What is the opera about, one may ask? The interpretive focus in *Radamisto* may be on the struggle to replace the rule of power and the military by diplomacy, cooperation, and compassion; alternatively, it can be regarded as the testing of marital love and the conflict between love of family and duty to a spouse.

Radamisto is one of the finest examples of Handel's contribution to the Italian style of *opera seria*. Polissena, unswerving in her love for her undeserving, tyrannical husband, and Zenobia, who is passionately in love with her husband Radamisto, are two of his most outstanding creations. In the Baroque tradition, the characters express the emotions they are feeling. Polissena's opening cavatina therefore is one of restrained despair at being neglected by her husband. She later sings of gentle devotion. By the end, however, the rejected wife turns from her unfaithful husband and sings a dramatic aria of anger and pain in "Sposo ingrato" (Ungrateful husband). Radamisto's first aria, "Cara sposa" (Dearest wife), is filled with love for his wife, which shifts quickly to heroic resolution. Later, "Ombra cara" (Dear shade), Radamisto's profound lament as he mourns his wife, is a dark, melancholic piece in a minor key. Zenobia's determination to remain faithful and resist the enemy at any cost is clear in her first aria, "Son contenta di morire" (I am happy to die). The warlike Tiridate is presented vigorously in three arias with brass accompaniment featuring a trumpet in his battle aria "Stragi, morte." Handel introduces two horns, instruments new to England at the time, in the aria "Alzo al volo."

The Baroque style conforms to a formula in which the exposition or recitatives, the story-telling parts, alternate with reflection in the arias. The recitatives are typically declaimed so the dialogue is clear, with minimal accompaniment. At the end of each scene a principal character reflects on what he or she has just experienced, and sings of just one emotion, becoming, in a sense, the personification of that emotion, whether it be love, hate, anger, revenge, despair, or sorrow. The Doctrine of the Affections, which proposed that music can arouse a variety of specific emotions in the listener, was an important component of the Baroque style. By making use of the proper procedure, the composer could create a piece of music capable of producing a particular emotional response in the listener. Musicians of the Baroque believed that if music was the physical embodiment of feelings, moods, and emotions, then one musical idea should be linked to only one emotion.

The *da capo* arias are the vehicles by which these emotions are expressed, one at a time, and generally at some length. The *da capo* aria introduces a theme which is followed by a second theme, then returns to the first (*da capo*, from the head) in an ABA form, generally with ornaments and embellishments. The ornamentation, runs, and trills in the repeat sections of the *da capo* arias were the most important and exciting feature of the Baroque style. At the time, singers wrote their own ornamentation to show off their voices to best advantage. Today ornamentation is generally a collaborative process between singer and conductor, although occasionally the conductor alone decides how the *da capo* embellishments should be performed. In an odd convention that challenges dramatic continuity, when an aria ended a scene, the singer would usually leave the stage in what came to be called an "exit aria."

In the 18th-century, if a singer did not like an aria, the composer – Handel included – was obliged to rewrite it until the singer was satisfied. If the singer was still unhappy, he or she would take the offending music to another composer and sing a replacement aria instead. Some singers had one or more so-called tailor-made "suitcase" arias, which they took out of the suitcase at every new venue and sang regardless of their suitability to the opera at hand. So 18th-century scores were never absolute. Even the most beautiful arias were improvised. These alterations could include more high notes if the castrato or soprano didn't think there were enough of them, florid embellishments to show off the singer's vocal acrobatics, and even fundamental changes in the melody line. By Mozart's time, these ornate sections were written down by the composer, and the singers were expected to perform the written score without deviation.

The orchestra of the Baroque was made up predominantly of strings, but Handel also featured horns, trumpets, and other brass instruments, along with a strong woodwind section with flutes, oboes, and bassoon. The harpsichord was the leading instrument of the ensemble which typically comprised from 25 to 40 musicians.

Confusion over voices and gender is an inevitable and intriguing aspect of Baroque opera. Castrati sang women's roles, just as, subsequently, women played (and still play) male roles in what are called pants or trouser roles. Tigrane, for example, the prince in *Radamisto*, is sung by a soprano in the Santa Fe production.

What was it that made the castrati so appealing to 17th- and 18th-century audiences? How did that style of singing come about, and how did that sound evolve into the countertenor of today?

The castrato phenomenon began in Italy in the 1600s. The castrato, called "musico" at the time, was a male with a pure, child-like soprano voice. Occasionally an endocrinological condition prevented such a boy from ever reaching sexual maturity, but usually it was castration that brought about the extraordinary voice in which the high vocal range of childhood was retained. The "operation" was performed typically when the boy was 8 to 10 years of age. Castrati often grew to be very tall with long bones and especially long ribs, which gave them unrivaled lung capacity and breath control. Their voices were extremely flexible, and intensive training further enhanced these physiological changes. The training of these adolescents was rigorous; they were forced to sing many hours a day to develop a perfect technique with vocal flexibility and power that no other singer could match. Something like four thousand boys were castrated annually in the 1720s and 30s in the service of art. The castrati were also popular in Germany and were, without doubt, the stars of the opera in England in the 18th century. The French never approved; Voltaire and Rousseau said castrati were "an offence against nature."

Castrati first appeared in Italy in church choirs in the early 1600s and, by the end of the century, were singing in the Pope's personal choir in the Sistine Chapel. Women were banned from church choirs at the time; as justification the Catholic Church quoted Corinthians 1.14.34, "Let your women keep silence in church." Evidently the Church fathers felt that castration of young boys was preferable to having women sing in church. It is a historical fact that the phenomenon of castrati both started and ended in church choirs. The last castrato sang in 1903, when the Vatican finally gave up the practice.

In one of the earliest operas, Monteverdi's *Orfeo* of 1607, all the principal roles, both male and female, were sung by castrati. Throughout the 18th century this was the preferred voice; baritones and tenors only came into their own following the demise of the castrati. These singers were wildly popular and earned exorbitant fees. Hysteria reigned in theatres where they appeared, with an atmosphere of wild adulation not unlike that of a Beatles concert in the 1960s. Farinelli, who sang for a rival opera company in Handel's time, was considered the greatest castrato of all. These men were reputed to be attractive sexually for both their mystery and because they could not get a woman pregnant. In those days of no birth control, that fact mattered.

A 1735 satirical pamphlet commented:
> *Who would not be unmann'd to gain,*
> *What they with so much ease obtain,*
> *For tho' they lose the power of harm,*
> *The women know they yet can charm.*

Since most Baroque operas were about gods and mythological events, the de-sexed, almost hermaphrodite castrato voice seemed appropriate. The unusual, fascinating sound of this voice was all part of the artificiality of the art form. Extremes in staging, sets, and costumes reflected the taste of the times; men wore costumes of ornate richness with great wigs and helmets with flowing plumes. The castrato voice expressed the extravagant spirit of the Baroque. When the bubble burst, as it did when *The Beggar's Opera* appeared in 1728, a style of opera and a way of life came to an abrupt end. In a way, the castrati brought about their own downfall with their outrageous behavior. If a castrato found that the theatre was filled with his supporters, it was entirely possible that he would play only to his friends, improvising the music and completely confusing the orchestra. If he were bored while another singer held the stage he might take snuff, mutter critical remarks about the other singer, and even go over to the stage boxes to chat and visit with friends during a rival's aria.

The castrati era in opera lasted through Mozart's time (Lucio Cinna in *Lucio Silla* was composed for a castrato, as was Idamante in *Idomeneo*). A Meyerbeer opera performed in Venice in 1824 was said to present one of the last appearances of a castrato on stage. In London in 1825, marking a complete reversal of the rave receptions they once received, a castrato was described as "a travesty of nature." These voices were gradually replaced, first by women singers, and then by the heroic tenor voice. In 1870 Italy banned the practice of castration (which in fact had always been illegal).

The life of Francesco Bernardi, (1686 - 1758) known as Senesino, demonstrates well the career of a successful castrato. Born to a barber/surgeon in Siena, he sang in the cathedral choir and underwent the knife in 1699 at the comparatively late age of 13. Senesino was subjected to a rigorous musical training and then made his debut in 1707 in Venice. He quickly acquired a major reputation and was soon singing all over Europe. His voice, it was reported, was "powerful, clear, sweet and equal, a contralto with perfect intonation." His elocution was unrivaled.

Senesino fell out with the Dresden opera company in 1719 when he refused to sing an aria assigned to him, going so far as to tear up the score in the heat of the argument. He was fired. Handel, arriving in Dresden soon after this drama, contracted him as *primo uomo* for the new Royal Academy for what was then a vast amount of money. Handel took on the tempestuous castrato and his tantrums because he was an outstanding singer. In December 1720, Senesino made his London debut singing Radamisto and enjoyed a resounding success.

He stayed in London for 16 exciting years, during which time he built a reputation for further tantrums and angry tirades; yet he found friends amongst the highest levels of society, and amassed a fine art collection. Although he created 17 leading roles for Handel, their relationship was always stormy. "One (Handel) was perfectly refractory, the other equally outrageous," wrote John Mainwaring, Handel's earliest biographer. Following the collapse of the Royal Academy, Senesino sang abroad for a while, then returned to London to sing once more for Handel.

In 1733 their animosity became so great that Senesino, to Handel's fury, joined the rival company, Opera of the Nobility. There Senesino sang alongside the most well-known castrato of all, Farinelli. Their first meeting on stage led to a famous incident, when Senesino played a furious tyrant and Farinelli an unfortunate hero in chains. In the course of the first aria, the captive so softened the heart of the tyrant, that Senesino, forgetting his role, ran to Farinelli and embraced him. Relations were not always so cordial, however; sopranos and castrati alike spent much of their time trying to upstage one another with scandalous, outrageous behavior (which the public, of course, adored). Senesino finally left England in 1736 and sang a few more years in Italy before retiring to Siena, his hometown, where he built a fine house and filled it with the art he had collected over the years.

Following the age of the castrati, young male roles were first sung by women as pants roles, but that too is now changing as countertenors take on these roles. The countertenor is an adult male who sings in the alto, mezzo, or soprano range – without having surgery. The voice is similar in placement to that of a mezzo, between tenor and alto pitch. It is still disputed whether the countertenor is an extended tenor voice or a falsettist. A countertenor who sings soprano roles may be called a sopranist. In the 20th-century countertenors, like the castrati before them, sang mainly in cathedral choirs and early music ensembles. In a renaissance of early music in the 1950s and 60s, Alfred Deller, an "alto" in St. Paul's Cathedral choir in London, brought the countertenor sound to the attention of the public. Benjamin Britten composed Oberon for Deller in his *Midsummer Night's Dream* in 1960. Today countertenors can be heard singing many forms of classical repertoire, including the title role in Philip Glass's *Akhanaten*, and Trinculo in Thomas Adès *The Tempest* which had its American premiere in Santa Fe in 2006.

Radamisto, sung by a soprano in the original version, still may be sung by a woman. A 2005 EMI recording features mezzo-soprano Joyce di Donato in the title role. In the Santa Fe production, David Daniels, considered the leading countertenor of our time, will sing Radamisto. He is known for his warm, expressive voice, his impeccable musicianship, and dramatic flair. Singer Stephanie Blythe praised Daniels for "his beauty of tone, honesty of delivery, and connection to the text." When she sings with Daniels, she said, she forgets he has "this different voice." Daniels was a not very successful tenor until he discovered his countertenor voice. With coaching and the support of George Shirley at the University of Michigan, he changed his *fach* (voice category) and achieved overnight fame when he sang Sesto in Handel's *Julius Caesar* at the Metropolitan Opera in the early 1990s.

Daniels says, "I don't think my voice is feminine – though I understand that is probably the best way to describe it. Anyone watching me producing the sound does, I'm sure, pick up on an essentially masculine quality. Right now I want to do more music that is not typically associated with the countertenor voice, and do it well.... I think it is imperative to have contemporary composers write for us as a voice type. We're here to stay."

In Santa Fe, Daniels will team with conductor Harry Bicket and director David Alden, both of whom he has worked with many times and of whom he thinks very highly. Harry Bicket hails from England and has developed an international reputation as an interpreter of the Baroque. Bicket conducted during the 1960s and 70s, the years of the Handel revival, and recalls, "There were wars over style, pitch, period, authentic instruments, everything Baroque. The first point you have to make with Handel is that the music exists because of the words, not the other way around." Bicket explains, "The music is Handel's response to the text, the characters, and the dramatic situation. When you spend as much as ten minutes listening to a *da capo* aria which may only have two sentences, then it's important to make those words live in every possible variation."

The Baroque, and particularly Handel, are enjoying a revival in our time, albeit with modernist and provocative productions. Director David Alden's interpretation of this 300-year-old work will be spectacular. Remaining true to the original source set in Armenia, Alden places the opera in the exotic world of ancient Persia with vibrant colors, costumes and sets, even mirrored floors and walls made of laminate. The Baroque loved spectacle and this 21st-century production continues the tradition.

Characters

Radamisto, son of Farasmane	Counter tenor
Polissena, daughter of Farasmane, and wife of Tiridate	Soprano
Zenobia, wife of Radamisto	Mezzo-soprano
Tigrane, Prince of Pontus	Soprano, a pants role
Tiridate, King of Armenia	Tenor
Farasmane, King of Thrace	Bass

Bibliography

Daniels, David. *Sento Amor*. Virgin Veritas CD 724354536526, 1999.

Giles, Patrick. "When Harry met Handel." *Opera News*, Dec. 2004.

Hogwood, Christopher, *Handel*. New York: Thames and Hudson, 1988.

Sadie, Stanley, ed. *The New Grove Dictionary of Opera*. London: Macmillan Reference Ltd., 1992.

Adriana Mater

Kaija Saariaho

"Will my son be Cain or Abel?" must be the cry of countless raped and pregnant women. Adriana Mater's cry rises out of contemporary reality in this tough story about a young woman who is raped and becomes pregnant by a soldier from her own village in a time of war. Not a likely scenario for an opera. Emerging, however, from the creative spirit of Finnish composer Kaija Saariaho, with a libretto by the Lebanese writer Amin Maalouf, this new work brings the tragedy of women like Adriana into clear focus while connecting her to innumerable others who suffered similar fates over time.

Kaija Saariaho comes to this material first and foremost as a mother, one who wondered, as women have always done, about the heart beating so close to her own while she was pregnant. Amin Maalouf brings to the opera a sense of mourning for Beirut, the city of his birth, along with memories of his days as a war correspondent. Composer and librettist blend their life experiences in this very immediate, personal exploration of the universal subjects of rape, motherhood, and war.

Maalouf first collaborated with Saariaho on her 2000 opera *L'Amour de loin*, which tells of the love of a 12th-century princely troubadour and his lady, who lives in a tower across the sea at the time of the Crusades. *L'Amour de loin* speaks of a distant love; the love found in *Adriana Mater* is the all-encompassing love between mother and son, a raped woman and the offspring of a rapist. The opera revolves around Adriana's agonized question: Will her son inherit her blood, her eyes, her voice and hands, or will he express the violence of his father? She must wait for him to grow up to learn the answer.

Adriana Mater is set in an undetermined place and time, but is generally regarded as taking place somewhere in Eastern Europe in the present day. The seven scenes of the two-act opera are connected by musical bridges as time moves from Adriana as a young woman before the war, to the time of the rape and into her pregnancy. After the intermission, the story picks up when her son, Yonas, is 17. The set throughout is the home and street where Adriana and her sister Refka live.

In the opening of the opera, strong, dissonant, siren-like eight-note chords marked *disperato,* set the scene in a sea of amorphous sound. The large, unseen chorus intones, chants, and reinforces the story throughout. The dark sounds of the opening give way to moments of rare beauty as the characters begin to emerge; the tuba blares forth when the action is barbarous, a clarinet describes Adriana. The initial feeling is one of foreboding, of dusk on a gray day before the outbreak of war in a small, insignificant village.

Adriana sits outside her house singing a traditional song that expresses the hopes and dreams of a young woman: "When the eyes of the city close, I reveal the voice I gathered in an autumn garden and pressed in the pages of a book."

A young man, Tsargo, approaches, holding a bottle, obviously drunk. He stands unsteadily between Adriana and the door of her house. Accompanied by the timpani, Tsargo complains, "Adriana doesn't know me now!" Annoyed, Adriana suggests he get drunk somewhere else; she might talk to him when he is sober. He taunts her, "If I were rich as well as drunk, you would invite me in." She mimes a scene in which, if he were sober, the way would not be barred to him. In a waking dream, she describes how they could be together, then, coming out of her reverie, insists, "But that day will never come." To a wailing from the orchestra, the rejected Tsargo moves away from the door, slides down to the ground and continues drinking, grumbling to himself.

Adriana enters the house. Her older sister Refka has observed this conversation through the window and criticizes Adriana, telling her she should have nothing to do with Tsargo. Adriana feels only contempt for him, not fear, she tells her sister. She will not succumb to "the fear women have been taught to feel since Eve." Adriana remembers how, at the fair the previous summer, she danced one dance with Tsargo, a shy boy, and how part of her feels some compassion for him.

Asleep, later that night, the three protagonists share a dream in which Tsargo, in his best clothes, knocks on Adriana's door. He has come to take her to the dance. She goes to take his arm but finds it has turned into a bottle, which drops and smashes on the ground. Adriana bursts out laughing. In the street outside, Tsargo has the same dream and now wakes and moves off, muttering threats at the laughing Adriana. The voices of the chorus describe the dream and interact with the voices of the individual characters, ending the scene intoning, "*Damné, damné, damné.*"

The next scene is set in wartime. A very different Tsargo, now a local leader, strides across the stage to knock on Adriana's door. He carries a weapon and is followed by his men. He demands that Adriana let him in, he needs to go up on her roof to look for the enemy. Adriana opens the door a little, barring his way: "There are other houses with higher roofs, Tsargo." She will not let him in. Tsargo threatens her, tries to frighten her, but she is determined: "War shall never enter into my house." She cries out that he, his thugs, and the enemy are all scoundrels. At last Tsargo loses his temper and forces his way into the dark interior of the house. Adriana shrieks "No! No! No!" Timpani and percussion take the part of the violent man as Tsargo assaults Adriana in a brutal section of music, in which we hear the rape but do not witness it. The chorus echoes the desperate cries of "No! No!" from Adriana until, abruptly, the music and the torment end.

A long orchestral interlude takes us from this violent scene to a calmer time a few months later, when the war has ended. The pregnant Adriana talks with her sister Refka, who reproaches her for ever having talked to Tsargo. Refka is also upset that Adriana has chosen to keep the child. She reproaches herself for not being home the night Adriana was attacked. Adriana believes that her unborn child, whose heart beats so close to her own, will be like her. Refka tells her sister about a dream, which is replayed in slow motion as the voices of the chorus mingle and overlap with the voices in the dream. Refka saw herself walking in the streets among burning houses in wartime. People were dying all around her, and they all had the same face. Suddenly she saw Adriana lying on the ground and called to her. Adriana said, "Can't you see I'm giving birth?" Refka has to get flowers for her sister and asks everyone where she can find them. She runs into two men, one old, one young. The old man holds his hands up in the air, the younger one aims a weapon at him. Refka asks for flowers. The young man turns and says, "Are you mad? Looking for flowers in the middle of a war? Wake up!"

The dream fades and the sisters wonder what it means, this glimpse of what is to come. Refka leaves and Adriana sings of her worry that the child she carries has two strains of blood, hers and Tsargo's. She loves her child as only a pregnant woman can and asks despairingly, "Who is it I carry? Who is it I feed? Which will my child turn out to be – Cain or Abel?" High strings and gentle woodwinds accompany Adriana's voice as she calmly asks the question, but then the sound gradually builds, conveying her inner turmoil and anguish as the curtain falls on the first act.

At the beginning of Act II, 17 years later, Yonas, Adriana's son, bursts furiously onto the stage. He has found out from the villagers that his father was not a hero who died defending him and his mother, as he had been led to believe all those years; his father was a monster, he is alive, and is called Tsargo. Yonas wants to kill him. Adriana is upset by his anger. She sought to protect him, she says, by hiding the truth until he was grown. She admits that she was wrong, but she had been young, hurt, and frightened. She summons up her courage to ask, "At what age should I have told my son I was raped and the rapist was his father?"

Adriana tells Yonas the story: Tsargo was a nobody who drank too much; then came the war, and all the young men acted as if they'd been "born again, unfettered, above the law, masters of the streets, the law and the nights, masters of women and things, dispensers of death." Tsargo and his soldiers roamed the streets, looting and killing. He made his followers call him Our Protector. Then he was wounded, the war ended, and Tsargo dared not return to the village. But Yonas, she tells her son, has not been affected by war, for she has protected him. The boy has only one response: "If he comes back, I'll kill him." Adriana, who has dreaded this moment since the night of the rape, cries out from the depths of her being, "My blood, your blood, his blood! [Blood] has no words, no memory, it can't tell you what to do.... Never speak to me again of your blood!"

Yonas sits on the floor with his head in his hands. His mother freezes as a third dream sequence unfolds. The stage directions describe the dream: A masked character [Yonas] tears off the masks of other people and throws them on a fire. "It's as if he is stripping them of their souls, and they collapse, one after another, in a blaze that at once destroys and purifies."

Refka enters and Yonas accosts her, asking wildly why she too had lied to him. Refka defends herself, relieved to know the boy knows the truth at last. She has news: Tsargo has been seen at his parents' old house in the village and intends to live there. Yonas swears he will kill the monster. Refka starts after him, then stops, wondering why Adriana is making no effort to prevent his going. "If he's going to kill him, then he'll kill him," Adriana says. Refka is frantic, wondering at her sister's cool complacence. Adriana repeats her words dispassionately, almost to herself, accompanied only by a little run-up on the clarinet. She will let her son go to the very brink of the act of murder, in the hope that he will pull back in time. The decision, the instinct driving him, must be his alone. This is the moment of truth she has dreaded since that fateful night. A throbbing timpani suggests, with the brass, the inevitability of what is to come.

Percussion, bells, timpani, and long, low, chanted notes from the chorus introduce the sixth scene. Adriana's presence is heard in the clarinet, which is her voice when she is not physically on stage. This pivotal scene is about her, about all she has suffered, and all she has loved in her son. An old man stands facing upstage. Yonas comes up behind him carrying a gun. Tsargo acknowledges who he is: "I too carried a weapon and used it to reinforce my voice with the same arrogance I sense in you...." Yonas tells his father his name. Tsargo barely reacts; he only remembers the beauty of Adriana when she was young. Yonas says he plans to kill him. Again Tsargo shows little reaction. A long painful pause follows, during which neither man quite knows how to proceed. Yonas tells the older man to turn around, as he will not strike from behind. Tsargo turns, and Yonas sees that he is blind. Tsargo moves towards the boy, arms outstretched as if to touch him. The boy recoils. Yonas cannot strike the blind man, so he desperately draws back as his father reaches for him. The crisis builds in the orchestra, then ends abruptly as Yonas retreats.

The final scene takes place moments later. The four characters are on stage but isolated from one another. Refka is anxious, Adriana filled with remorse, Yonas in despair, while Tsargo "wanders through his darkness in search of a death that eludes him." They are all in worlds of their own, caught somewhere between dream and reality. The bitter Adriana sings of the mask she has had to live behind, of how she has had to become tough. She sadly sings of the girl she once was, the girl who lives on in her soul. Refka weeps for her sister and blames herself. Tsargo seeks only death. Yonas, in fear and hate, asks if the blood of the killer runs in his veins. The chorus intones: "So many others. Other wars. Other births. Other crimes. Nothing can efface what happened that night." This quartet expresses the inter-related emotions and pain of the individual characters as they stand physically separated from one another until Tsargo wanders off, and Refka becomes a silent spectator as Adriana and Yonas move toward one another. Yonas begs his mother's forgiveness for not killing Tsargo. Adriana asks: If Tsargo were not blind, would Yonas have killed him? Yonas isn't sure. The chorus sings of how "The gates of Hell opened that night, and now the gates of Hell are closed again," because Adriana and Yonas chose not to continue the war or the killing. Their choice, affirming that vengeance is not the answer, means that they choose not be the conduit through which violence is perpetuated.

In her gripping final aria, Adriana tells Yonas of the long years when she hung onto the belief that he was hers, not his father's child. But she was always "tortured by doubt with the endless unrelenting question. What would happen when one day, weapon in hand, Yonas would confront his father?" She believes she now has the answer; Yonas did not kill, therefore he is hers. With infinite calmness Adriana, who feared for so many years that her son would take after his rapist father, now consoles that son: "We are not avenged, Yonas, we are saved. Put your arms around me. I need to rest my head on a man's shoulder." Something truly transformative happens in the last few moments of the opera, something deep and profound. It is not unlike the extraordinary mood of forgiveness that pervades the final moments of *The Marriage of Figaro*. There is resignation and extreme tenderness in Adriana's last words, as she lays her head on the shoulder of the boy now grown to be a man. The timpani, strings, her clarinet, and the now-quiet orchestra all dovetail to bring the opera to a haunting end as the lights slowly fade on mother and son. So ends a devastating story of our time, a realistic account of the horrors to be faced in a violent world.

In an *Opera Critic* interview with Michael Ellison, Kaija Saariaho talked about how she and Amin Maalouf chose this subject for the opera. She explained that she came to it with her experience as a mother, and that Maalouf brought his experience of war; together they devised the story. It is somewhat unique, even today, that the story of *Adriana Mater* is original, the shared creation of the composer, the librettist, and (in the early stages) director Peter Sellars. Once the story and the characters were agreed upon, Maalouf wrote a text that was quite linear. At Saariaho's suggestion he added the dream sequences, which gave her more freedom to develop the characters, each with their own orchestration and harmony, tempi and rhythmic behavior.

According to Maalouf, "The title was inscribed somewhere, and all we had to do was unveil it. *Adriana Mater* would work in all languages, there would be no need for translation." The opera is sung in French, the language in which it was written. Mater, the Latin word for mother, he said, evokes in this context the image of a challenged madonna.

The unseen chorus is a key component of the work. At the Paris premiere in 2006, at the Opera Bastille, the chorus was placed throughout the large theatre, providing a kind of surround-sound, enclosing the audience in the midst of their vocalizing, a complementary voice to the orchestra interpreting the feelings of the characters. Scenic designer George Tsypin designed a series of small domed houses standing among stone structures for the set. In the second act, following the war, these structures become ruins, a wasteland. This stark scene of domed houses is startlingly lit by washes of many vivid, revolving colors.

Kaija Saariaho studied composition in her native Finland before moving in 1982 to Paris, where she still lives with her own family. At IRCAM, the electronic music institute founded by Pierre Boulez, she created intriguing textures by blending instrumental and electronic timbres, and worked alongside composers of spectral or computer-generated music, a form she rarely uses now. Occasionally, she says, she returns to the techniques and analytical tools computers provide in order to analyze instrumental or vocal sounds and to discover fresh harmonic structures. Saariaho has composed in many genres: for chamber ensembles, for large orchestras, a ballet and, to date, two operas: *L'Amour de loin*, and *Adriana Mater*.

Saariaho works intuitively now; solutions come without effort, she says, and there are no electronic sounds in *Adriana Mater*. Themes of ideal beauty, forgiveness, and hope in the face of suffering are central to many of her compositions. "Music is so secret," she has said. "Our feelings are so secret and multi-faceted and so impossible to analyze." She wonders about the music we love and listen to: "Humanity and its relation to music is an unbelievably vast field. I have more and more the feeling that music is vast, limitless... [In music] I'm trying to communicate with other humans, looking for a way out of the horrible violence and suffering." She sees her operas as "meeting points" between her collaborators, the musicians and singers. Saariaho is aware that the opera, in performance, will bring things "we cannot analyze or expect. That is how art is...the mystery is there."

Amin Maalouf was born in Lebanon, and his first language was Arabic. He worked as a journalist for Beirut's leading newspaper, reporting from war-torn lands all over the world. In 1977, civil unrest in Lebanon forced him to leave his homeland for Paris, where he has lived ever since. His first book, *Les Croisades vues par les Arabes*, discussed the conflict between Islam and Christianity as seen through Arab eyes at the time of the Crusades. A master storyteller, Maalouf writes about "positive myths" and historical events in the Middle East. He said of *Adriana Mater*: "The line that divides humane behavior and barbaric behavior splits through each generation, and maybe every person." He makes the point that aggressive behavior can come not only from an enemy, but from one's own community, even one's neighbors.

Maalouf sought refuge from the horrors of war in fiction, choosing to write of troubled times throughout history. He belongs to a narrative tradition; if his stories are viewed as parables, he says, there is value in that, but it is not the intention that drives his work. He believes that cultural identity is at the heart of human conflict, identity made up of multiple elements. Resolving these elements among people of different faiths, races, and color is what he chooses to write about in his books. Maalouf feels that art, literature, music, and opera have a central role to play in combating the evils of the world. The purpose of art, he says, is an attempt to understand the harmonious existence of man through our differences and to fight intolerance and bestiality.

Adriana Mater will be performed in Finland in spring 2008 before its American premiere in Santa Fe in the summer. The Santa Fe production is directed by the mercurial Peter Sellars, who brings his own insightful interpretations to each new incarnation of a work. The Finnish mezzo-soprano Monica Groop, who sang the Pilgrim in Santa Fe's *L'Amour de loin,* sings Adriana; soprano Pia Freund is Refka; Canadian tenor Joseph Kaiser, fresh from successes at the Metropolitan Opera, sings Yonas; and bass Matthew Best sings Tsargo. The Spanish conductor Ernest Martinez Izquierdo will conduct *Adriana Mater* in the Helsinki spring production before leading the Santa Fe production in the summer.

Characters

Adriana	Mezzo-soprano
Refka, her sister	Soprano
Tsargo	Bass-baritone
Yonas, his son	Tenor

Bibliography

Ellison, Michael. "The Pains of Operatic Labour." The Opera Critic online, April 2006 (www.theoperacritic.com).

Personal communication, Kaija Saariaho, composer, January 2008.

Interview with Amin Maalouf. Opera National de Paris program, 2005-2006 season.

Ross, Alex. "Birth of a new opera." *The New Yorker,* April 24, 2006.

Maalouf, Amin. *Adriana Mater* libretto. G. Schirmer, Inc., New York, 2006.

The Marriage of Figaro

Wolfgang Amadeus Mozart

*Come, my dearest, and amid these sheltered trees,
I will wreathe thy brow with roses.*
— The Marriage of Figaro

*A*lways intrigued by human relationships, Mozart takes a bright, humorous look at the wedded state in *The Marriage of Figaro*. In 1781, in a letter to his father, he described his own reasons for wanting to get married: "The voice of nature speaks as loud in me as in others, yet I simply cannot live as most young men do these days [that is, promiscuously]. In the first place I have too much religion, in the second I have too great a love of my neighbor and too high a feeling of honor to seduce an innocent girl, thirdly, I have too much horror and disgust, too much dread and fear of diseases and too much care for my health to fool around with whores. I, who have not been accustomed to look after my own belongings, cannot think of anything more necessary to me than a wife." Mozart was preparing his father for news

Leopold would not welcome: the news of his engagement and forthcoming marriage to Constanze Weber.

Mozart felt sure he had found the right woman. "Constanze is not ugly, but at the same time far from beautiful," he wrote to Leopold. "She has no wit, but she has enough common sense to fulfill her duties as a wife and mother. I love her and she loves me with all her heart. Tell me whether I could wish myself a better wife?" Mozart appeared to have had realistic expectations of marriage, unclouded by romantic idealization or delusion. Leopold continued to disapprove of the match right up to the day of the wedding in August 1782 when he finally, begrudgingly, gave his consent. Mozart was 25, Constanze 19. Theirs was a playful, affectionate marriage, in spite of Constanze's feisty mother and Mozart's disapproving father. With Constanze, Mozart could enjoy some of the childhood he had missed while touring Europe as a child prodigy. Their marriage withstood the test of time (albeit a short time in Mozart's case), for he wrote to Constanze only five months before his death: "You can't imagine how I have been aching for you this long while. I can't describe what I have been feeling, a kind of emptiness which hurts me dreadfully, a kind of longing, which is never satisfied."

In 1786, Mozart lived with Constanze in Vienna under the protection of an enlightened monarch, Joseph II, at a time of great social change. The *ancien régime* was coming to an end, and the voice of the Age of Reason or Enlightenment was just beginning to be heard. In a radical departure from the past, the idea that marriage should be based on mutual need and affection, that both parties should have the right to freedom and love, was being freely discussed. An 18th-century English moral chapbook states, "No law obliges a man to marry, but he is obliged to love the woman he has taken in marriage. The husband first promises to love his wife, before she promises to obey him: and consequently since his love is the condition of her obedience, she need only obey if he is loving."

The plot of *The Marriage of Figaro* revolves around three very different marriages and Count Almaviva's passing attraction for Susanna, his wife's maidservant and fiancée of his valet, Figaro. The Count plans to seduce Susanna on the night before her wedding, in keeping with *le droit de seigneur*, the feudal right of the lord of the manor to have intercourse with his vassal's bride-to-be on the eve of the wedding. This medieval tradition was never actually law, but it was an ugly practice that servants were powerless to prevent. At the start of the opera Susanna tells Figaro that the Count, their master, is pursuing her in spite of the fact he has publicly repealed the old custom. "He'll send you off on some trip," she says, "Then in one bound he's in bed with me." The Count would like to reinstate his feudal rights but Susanna wants nothing to do with him.

The difficulty for the young couple lies not so much with *le droit de seigneur*, but with the Count's right to refuse Figaro permission to marry Susanna. Employing an ignoble and none-too-subtle form of blackmail, the Count makes it clear to Susanna that only if she succumbs to him will he give her a dowry and agree to her marriage.

Susanna, described as witty, clever, and high-spirited by her creator, the French playwright, Caron de Beaumarchais, is the one sane and faithful character in the entire opera. Beaumarchais states that Susanna commands our attention for two reasons: Pursued by a mighty seducer equipped with far more power than necessary to seduce a girl in her position, she immediately confides the Count's intentions to the two people most concerned with her, her mistress and her fiancé; secondly, Susanna is a woman whose every word communicates intelligence and devotion to duty. True to her love for Figaro, along the lines of Mozart's own fidelity to marriage, she outmaneuvers the rest of the cast so that, Master or no, the Count will be outwitted and she will be able to marry the man she loves.

The Countess and Susanna devise a plot to put a stop to the Count's philandering. The Count is to be humbled, Beaumarchais said, but never debased. In a delicious duettino, Susanna pretends to flirt shamelessly with the Count, promising to meet him later that night in the garden. He can't believe her change of heart. "Cruel one, why have you caused me thus to languish?" Susanna has a little fun here at the Count's expense when she flirtatiously replies, "A woman always needs time before she says yes," adding, in an aside to the audience, "Forgive my deception, you who truly love." The Count does not know that the woman he will meet in the garden later that night will be his wife disguised in Susanna's clothes.

So who is this unenlightened Count? He appears in *The Barber of Seville*, the first of three plays about the Figaro/Almaviva characters by Beaumarchais. In *Barber*, Count Almaviva employs the machinations of Figaro to gain access to the house of one Dr. Bartolo, who has a lively, pretty ward named Rosina. The Count is in love with Rosina, but it turns out that Dr. Bartolo has his own plans to marry her and is not at all happy with the intrusive Count. The passionate Almaviva is determined, and Rosina can't wait to marry him and get out of the house. By the end of the story they wed and escape into the joys of married life.

The Marriage of Figaro is set some three years later. Rosina, now the Countess Almaviva and mistress of the Count's ancestral home near Seville, is deeply in love with her husband, but he, bored with married life, is looking for a little diversion. He finds it on his doorstep, with Susanna. But Susanna refuses to be a victim of his tyranny. The Count is confused by her reaction. How can Susanna even think about rejecting him? After all, he is her lord and master. The servant problem was definitely getting out of hand. Figaro, his valet, is also argumentative and insubordinate. The great houses of the 18th century tried ineffectively to deal with the growing independence of servants by attempting to make them invisible, keeping them below stairs, giving them living quarters in basements or attics, requiring them to creep up and down concealed staircases and serve meals from dumb-waiters, an apt term.

The Marriage of Figaro takes place in the years immediately preceding the French Revolution, when the aristocracy was beginning to be concerned about this new master/servant conflict. The Count addresses the issue in his sole aria, "Vedrò mentr'io sospiro," in the third act: "Must I see a serf of mine happy while I am left to sigh? You were not born, bold fellow, to cause me torment and to laugh at my discomfiture."

The Almavivas' marriage is in trouble because both partners have different expectations of what marriage is all about. The Count believes it should be an ongoing sexual adventure; if his wife will not provide this adventure, he will seek it elsewhere. Near the end of Beaumarchais's play, when the Count believes he is wooing Susanna (really his wife in disguise), she asks, "What about love?" and he replies, "Love is no more than the story of one's heart; pleasure is the reality that brings me to your feet." He goes on: "Our wives think they do all that is necessary in loving us. They are so compliant, so acquiescent – always and all the time. They don't give enough attention to the art of holding our interest or reviving the charm of possession with the spice of variety." The disguised Countess swallows hard and goes on, "So it is all up to them?" "Of course," the Count replies, laughing, "Our part is to win them, theirs is to keep us." It is a pity that the opera does not include this crucial little exchange, for it makes the Count's plea for forgiveness and his wife's bestowal of it much more plausible. Once Almaviva and Rosina take off their disguises, their marriage may have a better chance since both now understand what is keeping them apart.

The Countess, unlike her husband, believes in romantic

love and expresses her feelings in two exquisite arias. When she first appears at the start of Act II, her aria is a prayer: "Porgi, amor" (Love, bring some relief to my sorrow, give me back my loved one or, in mercy, let me die.) This is the epitome not only of romantic love but of sentimental love, in which the fusion of love and death are synonymous. Somehow that connection works in tragedy, but not so well in *opera buffa*. In the style typical of 18th-century literature, the Countess feels sorry for herself and consoles herself with dreams of the past. She requires smelling salts, Susanna tells us, for she suffers from the vapors. Almaviva is losing interest in her, for she is no longer the vibrant, passionate woman with whom he fell in love. In her second aria, "Dove sono," the Countess reminisces about happier days and complains she is made to suffer even more by having to seek help from her servants. The music conveys the pain of a woman in a romantic novel, passive and submissive, a wronged wife. Mozart's music describes Rosina as sad, not tragic. There is a fine line here, for Mozart and his librettist, Lorenzo da Ponte, were notorious for presenting situations in which one cannot be sure whether parody or sincerity is intended. Most directors today approach the Countess as genuinely suffering and sad.

The Countess, however, pulls herself together and decides she is going to fight. She turns to her servants, Susanna and Figaro, to help her find a way to keep the affection of her once ardent, now philandering husband. Her true colors emerge when she rejects the role expected of a woman in her situation, placed on a pedestal as a revered image, beautiful, but cast aside and ignored. No longer the suffering romantic heroine, she plots, with Susanna, a clandestine meeting with the Count. She dictates a letter to her maidservant, a letter filled with her own nostalgic longing as she describes a secret meeting place under the pine trees, a place she has clearly been to before with the Count. In the letter, using her own sentimental language to entice and entrap her husband, she sets in motion a plan to win him back. The lovely duet for two sopranos, in which Rosina dictates the letter and Susanna repeats the words, "Che soave zeffiretto" (How sweet the breeze), reveals the unmistakable nobility, pluckiness, and courage of Rosina, one of Mozart's most magnificent characters.

The central marriage in both play and opera is, of course, that of Figaro and Susanna. Believing in a freely contracted marriage based on love rather than financial concerns or considerations of class, the enlightened Mozart embodies his ideas in the characters of these two, who must surmount all sorts of unforeseen obstacles before emerging victorious. Figaro, onetime barber and now valet to the Count, is in essence the voice of Beaumarchais, who was a wit, an adventurer, and a shrewd politician as well as a playwright. A member of the court of Louis XVI, he fought against injustice and inequality in the days before the French Revolution; ironically, his life was in danger after the Revolution because of his close ties to the court.

If Beaumarchais shocked Paris with his *Barber of Seville*, he shook it to its very foundations with *Le Mariage de Figaro*. He was censored for pitting a profligate nobleman against the nimblest brain in the city, the one and only Figaro who, while defending Susanna's and his rights, mocks his master. Beaumarchais wrote, "The battle lines are drawn between arrogation of power, breach of principle, recklessness, opportunism and everything else that makes seduction attractive, and the fire, wit and resourcefulness with which social inferiors parry the blows of their betters." In his first speech or cavatina, Figaro, furious with his master when Susanna tells him about the Count's designs on her, vents his anger, "Se vuol ballare" (If, my dear Count, you feel like dancing, it's I who'll call the tune). This aria closely paraphrases Beaumarchais: "No, my Lord Count, you shall not have her! Because you are a great nobleman you think you are a great genius. What have you done to deserve such advantages? Put yourself to the trouble of being born – nothing more."

There is an intriguing story about this cavatina and Sigmund Freud, who considered it the essence of rebellion. One cold, wet day Freud was singing it to himself as he paced up and down a station platform in Vienna. He was angry because he could not get a seat on the train. The song, he said later, expressed his rebellious feelings toward titled and official personages who could get compartments on the train by bribery. Then, he went on, all kinds of bold and revolutionary thoughts came to him, such as would fit themselves to the words of Figaro.

Figaro's devious plotting, however, has little success in *The Marriage of Figaro*. Most of his plans go awry, but Figaro, a man of the world, knows how that world turns. He says, in Beaumarchais, "There are truths one knows but dares not divulge, for not all truths can be spoken; those one can subscribe to without really believing, for not all truths are acceptable: lovers vows, statements made in drink, promises of men in high positions, the final word of our merchants – there's no end to them. There's only one truth worth relying on – my love for Susanna." When, near the end of both play and opera, Figaro mistakenly believes that Susanna really is going to meet the Count, he gives full rein to his anger in the aria "Aprite un po'quegli occhi" (Open your eyes, foolish men, look at these women, see them as they are. Goddesses, so called by the intoxicated senses.... They are witches who cast spells for our torment).

Susanna, Figaro's bride-to-be, is a survivor, well versed in the skills of social game-playing. Hers is the shoulder everyone cries on. She loves realistically, fights for what she believes in, and vocally supports everyone else in the opera in duets and trios and musical conversations until, in the final moments, she takes center stage and sings the glorious "Deh vieni." It is nighttime in the gardens of the Count. The air is fragrant with the perfumes of the flowers of southern Spain. The garden is filled with shadows and arbors or gazebos where lovers meet for clandestine rendezvous. Figaro hides behind a bush, believing he is about to witness his Susanna meeting the Count in the darkened garden. Susanna, who knows that Figaro doubts her and hopes to catch her in the act, sings her aria as if she were singing it to the Count, the irony is – and Mozart's music is filled with irony – she is singing both to and about Figaro. The andante mood of her song evokes stillness and a deep contentment, intimately revealing Susanna's love. This marriage, one feels, will be strong and stable, firmly rooted in mutual understanding and free of romantic and sentimental delusion.

The third couple in the opera is Marcellina and Bartolo, an unlikely pair. In *The Barber of Seville*, Dr. Bartolo was the guardian of Rosina, and Marcellina, onetime governess to Rosina, is now housekeeper to the Count. Marcellina complains to Dr. Bartolo that she has rights. In her hand she holds a contract with Figaro, who had borrowed a sizeable sum of money from her and who, the contract states, must marry her if he does not repay the money. Aware of Figaro's plan to marry Susanna, Marcellina is determined to see justice done and marry Figaro herself. Bartolo eagerly agrees to help her; he has his own axe to grind with Figaro over Rosina's marriage to the Count. Marcellina's angry denounciation of Figaro fits nicely into the Count's plans as well. If Susanna agrees to his proposals, the Count will give her and Figaro a dowry that would pay off the debt to Marcellina. But if Susanna will not acquiesce, the Count will stop the marriage by withholding the dowry.

Marcellina's contract becomes null and void, however, when it is revealed, with high comedy, that Figaro cannot be her husband because he is her son. If he is her son, then who is his father? To the amazement of all, it is Bartolo who, 30 years before, got Marcellina pregnant but did not marry her. Suddenly Marcellina does a comic about-face. Up to this moment in the opera she has been portrayed as an older, jealous woman; she now becomes a victim, the personification of virtue betrayed. In lines from Beaumarchais, Marcellina lets Bartolo have it on behalf of all abandoned women: "What can a young girl do at an age when we are beset by illusions, inexperience, and necessity, when seducers besiege us and want to stab us in the back? You men, lost to all sense of obligation, stigmatize with your contempt the playthings of your passions, your unfortunate victims." She gives voice to all the pent-up anger of women of her time. Her Act IV aria (often cut in production these days) expresses these sentiments: "We, members of the female sex, are victims of the men we love." Given this turn of events, Bartolo, publicly named as Figaro's father, agrees to marry Marcellina, saying, ungraciously: "He's my son, you are my consort. We'll get married when you wish."

Cherubino, a young page from a good family, serves in the Almaviva household in order to be educated in manners. The education he receives, however, is probably not the one his parents had in mind, for Cherubino is in love with love, and with every woman in the opera. He is caught by the Count flirting with Barbarina, the gardener's daughter. He flirts with Susanna in her room and has to hide quickly when the Count appears unexpectedly. Yet another time, he is found in the Countess's rooms in a state of undress, declaring his love for her by way of the song, "Voi che sapete." In this arietta Cherubino describes his nascent feelings of love: "I have a feeling, full of desire, which now is pleasure, now torment. My spirit all ablaze, next moment I turn to ice." He is devastated when the Count, to get him out of the way, assigns him a commission in the army and orders him to leave at once.

His very name a diminutive of the angelic cherubs of love, Cherubino disturbs the hearts and dreams of the women in the opera. His first intimations of love are described in Mozart's music as quiet desire, quiet longing, and quiet ecstasy. Desire, in Cherubino, is a mere presentiment, for he only dreams of love.

Mozart expresses many aspects of love in this opera, the first of three on which he collaborated with the colorful Lorenzo da Ponte. Both men struggled for recognition when they first arrived in Vienna; Mozart had no patron, and although da Ponte had been named Court Poet by the Emperor, his first libretto for Antonio Salieri had been a failure – he was a poet and had no idea how to write a libretto.

Mozart's earlier opera, *The Abduction from the Seraglio*, had been a success, but he was working freelance – unheard of at the time – and life was not easy. He wanted to compose an *opera buffa* based on Beaumarchais's French play, *Le Mariage de Figaro*, and da Ponte agreed to write the libretto. The work was written and composed quickly, over the period of a few months in 1786, and in secret, for both men feared that the intrigue, scandals, and sheer jealous rivalry of the opera milieu at court would sabotage the opera. Da Ponte went himself to propose the subject to the Emperor, who had already banned the play. He asked Mozart to play the score for him, and on hearing it, he pronounced his approval and the opera went into rehearsal at the Burgtheater, much to the annoyance of the court officials.

Mozart's genius blossomed now that he had a competent librettist to work with. The lively overture sets the mood, although it contains none of the opera's melodies. The opening duet between Figaro and Susanna is simple and direct, in a mood of affection and harmony. Recitatives carry the action of the plot forward, while the arias perfectly depict the feelings and thoughts of the characters. The opera includes many duets and ensembles; the 20-minute finale to Act I is a complete work in itself, starting as a duet and building to a septet in seven major key changes with the tempi moving from andante to prestissimo. The music flows unbroken, responding to every twist and turn of the lively plot, encompassing the whole in a mood of enchantment. This is Mozart at his best, a perfect example of the marriage of words and music.

Lorenzo da Ponte had fully established himself at the court of Vienna by the time Mozart approached him about *The Marriage of Figaro.* He was so busy that, when the Emperor asked him how he managed all his work, (he was writing three operas simultaneously for Salieri, Mozart, and Martin y Soler), he responded, "I write in the evening for Mozart, mornings I shall work for Martin, my afternoons will be for Salieri. I sit down at my table and do not leave it for 12 hours at a stretch. A beautiful girl of 16 lived in the house with her mother. She would come to my room at the sound of the bell. To tell the truth, I rang the bell quite often, especially at moments when I felt my inspiration flagging. (I should have preferred to love her only as a daughter, but...)."

Da Ponte, a poor Jewish boy who became a Catholic priest and a man of letters with a reputation for illicit love affairs and a love of gambling, was in his element in Vienna, basking in the Emperor's favor. When Joseph died, however, da Ponte had to leave Vienna. He married and immigrated to England and then, in 1805, to America, with his wife and children. Landing in New York, he became a grocer, ran a bookstore on Broadway, and later became the first professor of Italian literature at Columbia University. He led the campaign to build New York's first opera house and, in these twilight years, wrote his famous *Memoirs.* He died in 1838, 42 years after *The Marriage of Figaro*, and was buried in Queens.

The Marriage of Figaro, the creation of two brilliant men, is like a fireworks display, igniting in the grand manner as one set piece after another bursts into activity. While the conflict between Figaro and the Count is ongoing, we are diverted by new waves of excitement in the scenes between the

Countess and Susanna, Susanna and Cherubino, husbands and wives, Figaro and his newly-found mother, spectacular ensembles. All this activity explodes in a magnificent finale in which all the threads of the story are pulled together.

Mozart's biographer Michael Levey said of this tale of three marriages: "*The Marriage of Figaro* is a marriage of words and music which makes it probably the most perfect of all operas. Mozart was inspired by the vision of an ideal world where men may meet as equals rewarded by love from women who are also at least their equal. A marriage of love is meant to be a marriage of true minds as well." In the opera, all's well that ends well, of course, as bliss, harmony, and forgiveness grace the final great ensemble.

Characters

Count Almaviva	Baritone
Countess Almaviva	Soprano
Figaro, valet to the Count	Bass
Susanna, maid to the Countess	Soprano
Cherubino, page to the Count	Soprano
Dr. Bartolo	Bass
Marcellina, housekeeper	Soprano

Bibliography

Beaumarchais, Caron de. *The Barber of Seville* and *The Marriage of Figaro*. John Wood, trans. New York: Penguin, 1964.

Bolt, Rodney. *The Librettist of Venice.* Bloomsbury Publishing, New York, 2006.

Letters of Mozart. Hans Mersmann, ed. Dorset Press, New York, 1986.

Levey, Michael. *The Life and Death of Mozart.* Stein & Day, New York, 1972.

Osborne, Charles. *The Complete Operas of Mozart.* Da Capo Press, New York, 1978.

Falstaff

Giuseppe Verdi

Wearing a large silk hat slightly tilted back on his head, Giuseppe Verdi sits on a wicker chair by the prompter's box, a score in his left hand. He listens to the opening bars while his eyes, full of life, seem to follow an invisible web of melodies in the air, "I beg you, ladies and gentlemen, do not lapse into sentimentality! Gaiety! Gaiety! That is the essence of Falstaff...." During rehearsals his intense, deeply-set eyes lend his gray head, immersed in shadows, a severe, almost wild expression.

"From the beginning," he says. He raises his hands and beats time with extraordinary vigor. The Wives move forward. Then Maurel (Falstaff) sings, at first *mezza voce* so as not to tire his voice. Gradually he gets carried away in spite of himself, and finishes by tilting his hat at a great angle, acting the conquering, swaggering Falstaff as he will act it on opening night. When he has finished his lightning aria, "Quand'ero paggio...," the whole orchestra rises to its feet and applauds. Some hours later, Verdi pulls out his watch; it is nearly four o'clock in the afternoon. He makes a sign and everything stops. Applause breaks out as the Maestro rises, doffs his hat, and bows. The rehearsal is over. "Verdi was indefatigable, he's not a man, he's a force of nature," the theatre manager reported.

This, according to *Encounters with Verdi*, was how the octogenarian was loved and venerated at the time of writing *Falstaff*. There are many first-hand accounts of Verdi's thoughts on this, his final opera. "Do you know what *Falstaff* is?" he asked teasingly. "It is nothing other than an ancient Italian comedy, written in a very ancient language long before Shakespeare! Shakespeare took the material and added the character of Falstaff, who in the original comedy was a mere village braggart." In August 1893 he wrote to a colleague, "You have to hear *Falstaff*! I have orchestrated it very lightly. Everything springs from the ensemble. Great singers are not required but artists with good intentions, the singers must work as a team, they are not prima donnas but ordinary mortals." Verdi took a new approach in this opera, creating a personal type of continuous drama permeated with music in an overarching marriage of words and music. He was seeking uninterrupted theatre in which singing actors would collaborate with each other, rather than showing off their individual gifts; this style is familiar to audiences today.

Many friends and fellow artists wrote of their visits with Verdi in those latter years. At 86, Verdi was described as being "small, but not bent. His hair was still thick, and like his beard, gray but not yet white. From his face, in which time had scrawled a thousand wrinkles and lines, gleams a pair of eyes of wonderful warmth and compelling kindness; his whole being breathed perfect serenity."

Composer Jules Massenet described his 1894 visit to the Maestro's winter home at the Palazza Doria overlooking Genoa harbor: "I shall always see him bare-headed and upright beneath the scorching sun, showing me the iridescent town and the golden sea beneath us, with a gesture as proud as his genius and as simple as his beautiful artist's soul. It was almost an evocation of one of the great doges of the past, stretching over Genoa his powerful and beneficent hand."

Musicologist Arnaldo Bonaventura described Verdi's "deep-set, clear, sky-blue and sparkling eyes, which lit up his austere yet gentle and expressive face, framed by white hair and a flowing beard." During that visit, Verdi said to his friend, "Simplicity in art is everything, spontaneity and inspiration are crucial ... when the form is intricate, contorted and difficult, communication fails, and communication is the aim of art."

Giuseppe Verdi and William Shakespeare were two of the greatest communicators mankind has ever known. Verdi loved Shakespeare's work and composed operas on three of his plays: *Macbeth* in 1847, *Otello* in 1887, and *Falstaff* in 1893.

Verdi had planned a quiet retirement for himself and his wife, Giuseppina, at his home at Sant'Agata, but this was not to be. Giulio Ricordi, his longtime friend and publisher, introduced him to Arrigo Boito, a successful composer and librettist who was 30 years Verdi's junior. The two men tempted Verdi with a proposal for an opera based on Shakespeare's *Othello*. Verdi was immediately interested, and he and Boito created the enormously successful *Otello*.

Verdi again returned home and busied himself with the affairs of his farms and the Villanova Hospital, which he had designed, built, and paid for. Then, suddenly, Boito sent him a proposal and synopsis for an opera to be called *Falstaff*. Verdi, after re-reading the *Henry IV* plays and *The Merry Wives of Windsor*, wrote to Boito, "Excellent! Excellent! One could not do better than you have done. This *Falstaff* or *Merry Wives*, which two days ago was in the world of dreams, now takes shape and becomes reality!" He approved Boito's reduction of the number of characters and scenes; Boito was a master librettist with a deep understanding of music and poetry, along with an amazing ability to weave *Falstaff* together from not one but three of Shakespeare's plays. Boito and Verdi worked in close harmony, with none of the acrimony that had accompanied Verdi's earlier relationships with librettists. Verdi rarely changed Boito's lines, but set them at once to music.

Two days after his first enthusiasm, however, he wrote again to Boito. "In outlining *Falstaff*, have you thought of my enormous weight of years? What if I could not stand the strain? What if I failed to finish it?" But he ended the letter on an upbeat note, "What joy to be able to say to the public: 'Here we are again! Roll up!'" Boito at once replied, "I don't think you will find writing a comic opera tiring. The jokes and laughter of comedy exhilarate both mind and body. After having sounded all the shrieks and groans of the human heart, to finish with a mighty burst of laughter – that is to astonish the world." Verdi responded, "Amen. We'll write this *Falstaff* then!" But he insisted on complete secrecy; no one was to know they were working on a new opera.

Reducing Shakespeare's plays was not easy. Boito struggled: "To make the joyous comedy live with a natural and infectious gaiety is very, very difficult." Verdi wrote in August 1889, "I'm writing fugues, a comic fugue which could be in place in *Falstaff*." Neither of them could have guessed that the fugue would become the glorious finale of the opera.

By March 1890, Verdi had completed the first act and was in high spirits. But then progress slowed. A close friend, the conductor Muzio, died, and Verdi wrote, "As for Big Belly, I've done nothing more except for a few full stops or commas." In November, the Verdis, the Ricordis, and Boito dined together. At the end of the meal, Boito proposed a toast to "Big Belly!" The Ricordis looked confused "To *Falstaff*," he repeated. Still confused, Mrs. Ricordi turned to Verdi's wife. "A new opera?" Giuseppina nodded. The next day, the Italian newspapers announced to the world that Verdi was composing again. The secret was out.

Verdi insisted he was writing *Falstaff* purely for his own amusement. He wrote to Giulio Ricordi, "I began writing *Falstaff* simply to pass the time. The music is only half-sketched, much remains to be done." For his birthday, Ricordi and Boito sent Verdi a chocolate Falstaff with a round belly and dressed in Elizabethan costume. Verdi replied with good humor, "What a surprise! Big Belly! I've had no news of him for four months! He, meanwhile, dead drunk, has probably gone to sleep forever! Let him sleep! Why wake him? He might commit some piece of villainy that would shock the world." Then, "Falstaff is skinny, very skinny. Let's hope we can find some fat capon to fill his belly." And soon after this, "Big Belly is in a fair way to going mad. There are days when he won't budge but sleeps and is bad-tempered. At others he shouts, jumps, causes a devil of a rumpus. I let him indulge his whim a bit; if he goes on like this I'll put him in a muzzle and a straitjacket."

By June 1892, the three-act opera was ready for the publisher. Verdi insisted that he have full control of the engagement of singers, and even coached some of them in his home. Ricordi assured Verdi that he would have a free hand to organize the opera any way he chose at La Scala in Milan. Piano rehearsals under Verdi began in November, when the composer was 79 years of age. The first night – performed before royalty, government ministers, leading artists, and musicians – was a triumph. Verdi led Boito on stage many times to share the applause. Returning to the Grand Hotel, Verdi had to appear three more times on the balcony of his suite to acknowledge the cheers of the enthusiastic crowd below.

Who is this Falstaff who inspired such affection in Verdi, the character who brightened and gave focus to the great composer's later years? Shakespeare describes him thus:

"A fool and a jester who requires two and twenty yards of satin for a suit." Prince Hal, who becomes *Henry V* in the plays, says to Falstaff, "Have you not a moist eye, dry hand, yellow cheek, a white beard, a decreasing leg, and increasing belly? Is not your voice broken, your wind short, your chin double, your wit single and every part of you blasted with antiquity? And will you yet not call yourself young?" He is variously described by Shakespeare as "an amazing bundle of contrasts, a liar without malice, a lover of wine, women and song, the most irrepressible of mortals, a sanguine coward, this bed-presser, this huge hill of flesh." While these descriptions are hardly attractive, there is an undertone of affection in how Falstaff is perceived. Kevin Newbury, who directs Santa Fe's production, sees Falstaff as "fun-loving, vice-ridden, mischievous, larger-than-life, inherently theatrical."

In Shakespeare, the old villain, Sir John Falstaff, ran with a wild crowd that included the young Prince Hal. Later in *Henry V*, the Prince rejects his erstwhile friend. Falstaff's career does not end here, however, for a story persists that Queen Elizabeth, intrigued by this funny man, announced that she wanted to see Falstaff in love. Shakespeare set to work at once and wrote *The Merry Wives of Windsor* in just two weeks in 1601.

The Merry Wives was set in Windsor, a small town on the Thames at the foot of Windsor Castle. Boito brilliantly reduced the number of characters from the play, retaining the delightful wives, Mistresses Alice Ford and Meg Page; Alice's husband, Ford; their daughter, Nanetta, who is in love with Fenton, a young suitor; Mistress Quickly, who acts as a go-between; Bardolph and Pistol, followers of Falstaff; and Doctor Caius. The Santa Fe production will show country life in Windsor in the early 16th century; the goal of the production, director Newbury says, is to "Create a world true to Shakespeare's Elizabethen setting, and tell a story that is at once hilarious, beautiful, magical, and, ultimately, forgiving."

The story is not complicated. Sir John Falstaff, low on funds to support his extravagant lifestyle, sends identical love letters to the wives of two rich burghers in the hope of wheedling money out of them. The wives compare notes and, in a spirit of fun, decide to teach Falstaff a lesson. Alice Ford invites Falstaff to her home for an assignation, but after he arrives Meg Page shows up – as does Ford, Alice's jealous husband, who believes his wife is having an affair with Falstaff. Ford's appearance comes as a total surprise to the Merry Wives; this was not part of the plan. The chaos of this scene builds as the Wives stuff Falstaff into a laundry basket to hide him from Ford, then have the basket dumped out of the window into the river.

Momentarily chastened, Falstaff fortifies himself at the inn and, at Mistress Quickly's behest, agrees to another assignation with Alice Ford, this time at midnight in Windsor Park. The entire cast convenes at Herne's Oak dressed as magical fairies, pixies, and goblins that pinch and persecute the frightened Falstaff until he discovers who they really are, and everyone ends up laughing. In a delightful side plot, the young couple, Fenton and Nanetta, make the most of every opportunity to be together. Boito wanted to present the young pair "to sprinkle the whole comedy with their love, as one sprinkles sugar on a tart." Ford, Nanetta's father, does not want her to marry Fenton, but that problem works itself out in ways that only opera and Shakespeare can devise.

Falstaff abounds with fast and fleeting gems. There is no overture; we plunge right into the action at breakneck speed. Falstaff is discovered at the Garter Inn, enthroned in a great chair, the remains of a gargantuan meal laid out before him. He tells his followers, Bardolph and Pistol, that they are costing him too much as he calls for more wine and sings a eulogy to himself: "If Falstaff gets skinny no one will love him. In this paunch a thousand tongues cry out my name. This is my kingdom [patting his belly], I will increase it." When Bardolph and Pistol refuse to carry his love letters to Mistresses Ford and Page, he lectures them on the subject of honor.

Boito expertly wove together the lines for this aria from Shakespeare's plays. The great three-part monologue at once provides a sense of Falstaff's wit and cynicism. The first part describes how Falstaff sidesteps honor when it is convenient to achieve his own ends. In the second he asks, "What honor? Can honor fill your belly? No. Can honor set a broken leg? No. Honor is not a surgeon. What is it then? A word. What's in this word? Air, which flies away. A fine word" (*Bel costrutto*). He goes on, "Does a dead man know honor? No. Does it live then only with the living? Not even that, for it puffs up at flattery, pride corrupts it, slander sickens it. For me, I'll have no part of it." The monologue ends with the woodwinds laughing derisively at Falstaff's contemptuous dismissal of the subject of honor.

In the tidy garden of Mistress Ford's house, the two Wives discover they have been sent identical letters, and their musical conversation leads in to a remarkable ensemble. Ensembles had always been a Verdi speciality; in *Falstaff* he surpassed himself. The characters not only sing as individuals but also gather in groups that are themselves composed as musical entities. The Wives, Nanetta, and Mistress Quickly share and divide their individual lines in an unaccompanied quartet, then gradually come together and sing, as a group, in triplets. Next the five men, after conversing individually, sing together in a different tempo. The two groups are on either side of the stage and, by the end, Verdi has the women singing in a dancing triple rhythm while superimposing the men's music in double time, with amazing effect.

In another grouping in Act II, this time with four sets

of singers, Verdi has the whole ensemble sing together as they all do different things: Fenton and Nanetta sing to one another of love in a high sustained melody above the rest; the jealous Ford and his supporters search busily for Falstaff; the Wives sing as they pile dirty laundry on top of the fat knight; while Falstaff complains bitterly about suffocating in the basket. The total effect is multi-faceted, funny, and harmonious.

Falstaff's disreputable companions, Bardolph and Pistol, meet with him at the Garter Inn. Mistress Quickly is announced, she tells Falstaff that Alice Ford has agreed to meet him, comically addressing him as "Reverenza" and assuring him that he bewitches all women. "No witchcraft," he says, "only a certain personal charm." When Quickly leaves, the delighted Falstaff sings the great self-congratulatory aria, "Va, vecchio John" (Go, old John, all women are in a whirl to damn their souls for me), to music of immense self-satisfaction from strings, trumpets, trombones, bassoons, and timpani.

Bardolph then announces Ford, Alice's husband. Suspicious of his wife and Falstaff, Ford has come disguised as Mr. Fontana to find out what is going on. Wishing to test his wife's loyalty, he asks Sir John for help in seducing Alice. In a comic duet, the two men consider the subject of love. "Love, which never gives us peace our whole life through. [Love] is like a shadow which you flee, yet it follows you, and if you follow it – it flees!" Falstaff informs Mr. Fontana he has an assignation with Alice that very afternoon and proclaims, "If that lout [her husband] disturbs me, I'll cudgel him between his [cuckold's] horns." Later, Mr. Fontana (Ford) sings a furious aria: "Two enormous horns are sprouting from my head! My wife wantons, bringing shame upon my honor, my house, my bed." Needless to say, the orchestral horns are well to the fore in this nearly serious aria on the subject of jealousy.

During his rendezvous with Alice, Falstaff, who has all the great arias in the opera (the women have only one aria among them: Nanetta's, in the last act), sings the half-minute arietta "Quand'ero paggio," boasting, "When I was page to the Duke of Norfolk, I was slender, a mirage, light, firm, and gentle. So lean, lithe, and slender you could have slipped me through a ring." The scene ends in chaos, with Falstaff being unceremoniously dumped out of the window into the Thames.

The opening scene of the final act reveals a miserable Falstaff drying out after his soaking. "Thieving, rascally world," he complains. Then he calls for mulled wine and revives as the wine tingles through his body. This song to wine becomes, in Boito and Verdi:

> *Good wine chases away the gloomy thoughts of sorrow, from the lips it rises to the brain wakening the fairy smith of trills, a black cricket who sings in the reeling brain, waking to trills every fiber of the heart. A thrilling gladness which infects the happy globe and quivers through the entire world.*

Boito plays on the Italian words, describing how a little cricket *(grillo)* gets into a man's veins when he is drunk *(brillo)*, making his body thrill *(trillo)*. The idea of a gradually spreading warmth begins in the orchestra on an E natural trill played on a single flute. It is taken up by other instruments in unrelated keys, until the entire orchestra vibrates and trills in the key of E major.

By the end of the second act, the drama is virtually over. How to maintain the audience's interest for the final act? Verdi and Boito work magic by presenting an utterly fantastic scene in which the mood of the whole opera, while still humorous, changes from everyday hustle and bustle to enchantment.

As midnight strikes, a disguised Falstaff with antlers on his head appears in the forest to keep his second rendezvous with Alice. She appears, then disappears as the stage fills with magical fairies, goblins, and witches. Nanetta, as Queen of the fairies, calls up nymphs, sylphs, and sirens. Falstaff drops to the ground, terrified of being discovered by the fairy folk. The Merry Wives and a crowd of men arrive, all in fantastic costumes, and surround the prone Falstaff, pinching, poking, and generally torturing him. In Santa Fe, Herne's Oak is shown upended, its roots face the audience, and it moves slowly downstage to envelope the terrified Falstaff. The principals hurl insults at him: "Paunch like a pumpkin, brain of a bumpkin! Greatest of gluttons, burster of buttons! Breaker of benches, chaser of wenches! Infamous brawler, triple-chinned sprawler!" Falstaff pleads "Mi pento" (I repent), but to no avail, until Bardolph's disguise falls off and Falstaff recognizes him. The game is up, and Falstaff realizes what has happened: "I begin to see I've been an ass." The Merry Wives take off their masks. "Now, Sir John," Ford gloats, "who is the cuckold?"

Falstaff brushes himself off and sings, "The world is but a joke and man is born a clown." The subplots are quickly resolved, and Fenton is betrothed to Nanetta. The opera ends with the brilliant comic fugue, Verdi's final comment on his work, life, opera, and the stage: "Tutto nel mondo è burla" (The whole world is but a joke and man is born a clown, but he laughs best who sees to it that the last laugh falls to him).

Falstaff is a departure from everything Verdi had composed before. The music responds in meticulous detail to the libretto; the words and music feed one another, driving the comic aspects of the plot. The score is diverse and filled with color. Tunes are scattered throughout, fast and fleeting; the pacing is hectic, but hidden in the score are myriad treasures as Verdi plays with his mercurial characters. Sir John is one of the greatest comic characters in all literature. While it is true that this Prince of Rascals is humiliated and demeaned in both play and opera, a fine singer-actor will bring out the wit, vast spirit, and *joie de vivre* of Big Belly, allowing the audience to revel in the fun. In the mischievous cut and thrust of Verdi's rich score, and in Boito's tight libretto, one cannot fail to be thrilled by the sheer buoyancy of Falstaff.

Verdi must have put away his pen sadly after completing *Falstaff.* When he sent the finished score to Ricordi, he tucked a little note into the pages of the final act that read, "It's all finished. Go, go, old John. Go on your way for as long as you can. Amusing rogue, forever true beneath the masks you wear in different times and places. Go, go, on your way. Farewell." Thus did Verdi send the last child of his creative imagination on his way, and in so doing said a personal farewell to Falstaff, his colleagues, and his audiences, both then and now.

Characters

Sir John Falstaff	Baritone
Mistress Alice Ford	Soprano
Ford, her husband	Baritone
Nanetta, Alice's daughter	Soprano
Fenton, Nanetta's lover	Tenor
Mistress Meg Page	Mezzo-soprano
Mistress Quickly	Mezzo-soprano
Bardolph, follower of Falstaff	Tenor
Pistol, follower of Falstaff	Bass

Bibliography

Budden, Julian. *The Operas of Verdi*, vol. 3. Oxford University Press, 1973.

Cambridge Opera Handbooks. *Giuseppe Verdi: Falstaff*. James Hepokoski, ed. Cambridge University Press, 1983.

Encounters with Verdi. Marcello Conato, ed. Cornell University Press, 1984.

Goldovsky, Boris. *Good Afternoon, Ladies and Gentlemen*. Indiana University Press, 1984.

Parker, Roger, *Falstaff*. Stanley Sadie, ed. *New Grove Dictionary of Opera*. London: MacMillan Reference Ltd., 1998.

Phillips-Matz, Mary Jane. *Verdi, a Biography*. Oxford University Press, 1993.

William Shakespeare: The Complete Works. London: Collins Press, 1953.